Joseph Forgives His Brothers

Genesis 37, 39–45 for children

Written by Robert Baden
Illustrated by Chris Sharp

CONCORDIA PUBLISHING HOUSE · SAINT LOUIS

A man named Jacob had twelve sons
    In Israel long ago;
He loved the one named Joseph most
    And often told him so.

He made a richly colored robe
    That Joseph often wore.
His brothers didn't like the robe,
    Or that Dad loved Joseph more.

Then Joseph shared some dreams in which
His brothers bowed before him.
The others thought he'd gone too far
For them to just ignore him.

"I hate this boy," one brother said.
"He really makes me mad!
If Joseph disappeared," he said,
"I know that I'd be glad."

So they sold Joseph to some men
　　Who came along the way;
And these men took him as a slave
　　To Egypt that same day.

　　　　Poor Jacob thought his son was dead;
　　　　　　His brothers soon forgot him.
　　　　But God kept Joseph safely with
　　　　　　Potiphar, the man who bought him.

With God's help Joseph did so well
Each job his master gave
That Potiphar soon liked him more
Than any other slave.

Then Joseph was accused of sin,
    And soldiers quickly jailed him.
His master's wife had told a lie,
    But the Lord God never failed him.

In prison, Joseph helped explain
    The dreams of men around him;
And when Pharaoh had a dream,
    He searched him out and found him.

Joseph said that Pharaoh's dream
        Of cows and stalks with grain
Meant that Egypt land would thrive …
        Then have a lack of rain.

        Joseph said to store up food
                To have enough on hand.
        This pleased Pharaoh very much,
                And he put Joseph next in command!

It happened just as Joseph said:
    Crops grew for seven years.
But then came seven years of drought,
    Of hunger, pain, and tears.

    In Israel, Jacob and his sons
        Had also seen no rain;
    He sent them down to Egypt with
        Some money to buy grain.

When Joseph saw his brothers bowing
    At his feet, he cried.
They didn't know him then, of course,
    Because they thought he'd died.

He told them who he was, forgave them,
    Took them in his arms.
"God turned your evil deeds to good;
    He kept me safe from harm."

    The brothers hurried home and told
        Their father what had occurred;
    Old Jacob said, "I can't believe
        This good news that I've heard!"

    Jacob and his family left
        Their tents on desert sand
    To live in homes much better now,
        In Egypt—Joseph's land.

Dear Parents:

All children feel jealous of brothers and sisters at times. Use this story as an opportunity to assure each (or your only!) child of your love. Talk about times that make family members feel jealous and angry. How can you share God's love and forgiveness in those times?

Explain to your children that although Joseph was in terrible trouble—sold as a slave and put in jail—God worked through those trials to bring much good for Joseph and his family. Read Romans 8:28 with your family. "We know that in all things God works for the good of those who love Him, who have been called according to His purpose." Pray about a problem or concern your family has been having and ask God to work through it. He will bless you—just as He blessed Joseph and his family.

The Editor